HAUN' HAPPENINGS in Devon

Judy Chard

**additional material
by Sally and Chips Barber**

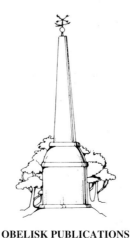

OBELISK PUBLICATIONS

ALSO AVAILABLE

Tales of the Unexplained in Devon, *Judy Chard*
Tales of the Teign, *Chips Barber and Judy Chard*
Burgh Island and Bigbury Bay, *Chips Barber and Judy Chard*
The Ghosts of Exeter, *Sally and Chips Barber*
Dark and Dastardly Dartmoor, *Sally and Chips Barber*
Ghastly and Ghostly Devon, *Sally and Chips Barber*
Weird and Wonderful Dartmoor, *Sally and Chips Barber*
The Ghosts of Torbay, *Deryck Seymour*
The Ghosts of Berry Pomeroy Castle, *Deryck Seymour*
The Ghosts of Brixham, *Graham Wyley*
The Ghosts of Totnes, *Bob Mann*
Ten Family Walks on Dartmoor, *Sally and Chips Barber*
Made in Devon, *Chips Barber and David FitzGerald*

For further details of these or any of our titles, please send an SAE to Obelisk Publications at the address below, or telephone Exeter 468556.

PLATE ACKNOWLEDGEMENTS
John Lynn for page 3
Mrs Naomi C. Feagans for page 32
All other photos by or belonging to Chips Barber
All drawings and cover by Jane Reynolds

*First published in 1988
as* The DevonAir Book of Haunted Happenings
*(ISBN 0 946651 21 3)
Reprinted in 1989 and 1991
This revised edition
(ISBN 1 899073 09 4)
published in 1994
by Obelisk Publications, 2 Church Hill, Pinhoe, Exeter, Devon
Typeset and Designed by Sally Barber
Printed in Great Britain by
Maslands Ltd, Tiverton, Devon*

INTRODUCTION

As a result of the popularity of my various books on the supernatural in Devon, and also of the various broadcasts on the subject I have done on local radio, I have made a further collection of hauntings in Devon, but with a slight difference because most of these are actually from people who have related them directly to me, either in person, over the telephone, or in a letter. As you will see, some have been very willing to have their names quoted, others have not, which is their prerogative, but in every case I feel they have been related with utter sincerity. As the late Theo Brown, an expert on folklore, said, "If people believe you are serious they will tell you things."

If some people appear more often than others, this is because they have been overtly generous in talking to me, but I would like to thank everyone who has contributed, given of their time and been generally helpful. I have tried to give as wide a selection as possible from my enormous hotch potch of material and to keep within the boundaries of Devon so they may be of local interest.

Perhaps it would be nice to start with a pure piece of fun because, after all, many ghosts and poltergeists do have a sense of humour!

For those who doubt the powers of the super-natural, this appeared in a local paper: a customer in a bookshop was buying a book on Zen Buddhism but the cash register refused to charge up a sale!

Chips Barber & Judy Chard get into the 'spirit' of Hallowe'en

GHOSTS WHICH GO GROWL!

Stover House at Newton Abbot is now a girls' school, but was once the home of John Seymour, Duke of Somerset. He was a great fox-hunting fanatic and bred the animals just to hunt them, in fact the fox pens are still to be seen at the back of the school, rather like dungeons! The Duke bred one fox that was to become renowned for its evasive tactics and was the downfall of many a so-called first class huntsman – no one could outwit its vanishing acts and so it became a legend in its day. This fox has of course been dead for over 100 years but its ghost has been seen often, sitting on the wall on the perimeter of the house on the main road near the Golf Club. It flings itself from the wall into the air in front of passing motorists, practically landing on the bonnet of the car. Some people have actually felt an impact with the car, it then vanishes to reappear on the same spot on the wall…

On the animal theme, I have my own experience. I had a black cocker spaniel who adored going out in the car until my husband changed the one we had for a green Alvis. Directly the dog saw it his hackles rose and he howled. Every time we wanted to go out I had to lift him into the car (whereas before he had jumped in), he even snapped at me a couple of times. Eventually the car was destroyed in a fire…

Mrs Jordan from Paignton told me about her little dog, whom she took a photograph of a few years ago, standing in the sea at Paignton. It was not during the summer months, so there was no question of any blown up rubber toy animal in the area, and there was certainly nothing visible in the sea at the time, but when she had the film developed, she was surprised to see, in the background behind Jason, a clear picture of a white sea-horse!

Another animal story came from Mrs Sherwood of Brixham. She and her husband bought a small cottage for their retirement in Brixham. Until the actual date for him to retire she spent her time redecorating the cottage, which was full of character with old beams and a large stone fireplace. A small curved staircase to the sitting room was boxed in, as is often the case in these old cottages that are modernised. She decided to open it up to make the room bigger. Another small cupboard was revealed with a door under the stairs. Inside it had deep grooves and scratch marks as if a dog had been shut inside.

One night, while her son and his family were staying with her, she was sleeping on the settee in the sitting room. She was awakened in the early hours of the morning by a scratching noise, which lasted about fifteen minutes. As it was light she got up and searched all the rooms but there was no animal anywhere.

The next morning she awoke again at dawn. As she lay there, admiring her wallpaper that she had put up the previous day, a small black dog walked out, literally, from the side of the settee. She hardly dared to breathe, feeling that if she did he would disappear. He stood looking straight into the fireplace. He had a lovely smooth shiny coat, and his eyes were alert and sparkling. The air was still, almost electric. Two women walked past the house, but their voices and footsteps seemed muffled. The dog turned and walked up the stairs. She clearly saw each paw rest on each stair. She looked hard at him as he went round the curve of the stairs. She could not see through him – he looked real and solid and full of life and was about the size of a Jack Russell but with longer legs. She waited to see if he would come down again but he didn't.

Opening the door of the sitting room she found the french doors open, which she had closed and locked before going to bed. She presumes that they were there in his day but the sitting room door was new so he would have just walked through it. The kitchen had been added, so that would have been part of the garden. They still live in the same cottage but have never seen him since.

DON'T WATCH THE BIRDIE!

There are of course many stories about black dogs on Dartmoor, of which most of us are heartily sick, but white birds occur too, and I think the White Bird of the Oxenhams has perhaps not had as much coverage as some of the other legends, and it is one I am frequently asked about.

The story began on a remote farm in the parish of Zeal Monachorum, the first records being in 1641. James Oxenham lived with his large family and in 1635 his eldest son John, aged about twenty-two and, from all accounts, a strong healthy man, suddenly died. Two days before he died he had seen a white bird hovering above him. Two days later his sister-in-law, Thomazine, also had a similar visitation and died. Later her sister, Rebeccah, aged eight, also saw this white bird and died, followed by the fourth member of the family, the baby of Thomazine.

The story continues with Margaret Oxenham who was the heiress to the property and was to marry a neighbouring landowner, Bertram. However, he became mad as a result of an accident and although for some time Margaret mourned him, later she was courted by Sir John of Roxamcave. On the wedding morning, as she made her preparations for the marriage, a white bird appeared and hovered over her. Later, as she stood by the altar, the deranged Bertram rushed in and stabbed her.

In the seventeenth century, events relating to the family became famous because James Howell in his "Familiar Letters" stated that in 1632 he had seen in a stonemason's in Fleet Street, a memorial tablet being engraved and destined for a church near Exeter. On it was recounted the appearance of the white bird before four Oxenham deaths. Unfortunately the marble tablet has never been seen since and it has been suggested its delivery was delayed by the upheavals of the Civil War, and it may eventually have been turned over and used for another memorial elsewhere.

But there have been further reports down the years – in 1743 William Oxenham, aged sixty-four, saw the bird fluttering outside his bedroom window. He defiantly announced that he would cheat it – but he died just the same. At Sidmouth between 1810 and 1821 another member of the family died in a house later replaced by Sidlands. The people who were in the room when he died knew nothing of the legend, but they saw a white bird fly across the room and vanish into a drawer! In 1873 Mr G. N. Oxenham died in Kensington. His nephew, Rev Henry Oxenham, said a week before his uncle's death he had seen a white bird fluttering outside the window. His daughter and a friend, who knew nothing of the tradition, opened the window and saw a white bird, larger than a pigeon, perched on a bush outside. Some workmen were trying to frighten it off without success. As he lay dying, his wife and the nurse heard flutterings as of a bird in the room.

Sarah Hewett, the Devon writer, tells how an Oxenham had recounted to her that the bird appeared to him in 1892 and, soon after, his father died.

Theo Brown said that in this century the bird has continued its dismal work although in 1969 she spoke to an old lady of the clan who was very sceptical and did not believe in the tradition, or that her uncle had seen the bird at a farm on the edge of Exmoor in 1919 when her father was dying! However, the late J. R. W. Coxhead, the writer, claimed to have heard of a more recent sighting in Canada.

NOW YOU SEE ME...

Mr Mason of Buckfastleigh once had a delivery round, which took him to many out-of-the-way houses on Dartmoor. One day, whilst negotiating a twisting narrow lane, between the Dart at Spitchwick and the hamlet of Leusdon, he saw a ghost. He said that the nature of the lane necessitated that he drove along it very slowly when, out of a gateway on his right hand side, came the figure of a man who strolled across the road in front of him and disappeared into the high hedged bank opposite. The hedge was as impenetrable as a wall!

The names in this next story have been changed. George was a long distance lorry driver who lived in a village outside of Exeter. One misty morning he left home at 4 am. A little way along the road he passed Jack, a local man who worked in a market garden, and gave him a wave. Across the road he noticed a stranger dressed in an old mac.

George was away for about three days. When he returned his mother prepared his tea and asked, conversationally, whether he had noticed anyone as he'd left the other morning. George said that he'd seen Jack, and also noticed a stranger. George's mother was so shaken at this, she dropped the cup she was holding. It transpired that Jack had been scared out of his wits by a 'ghost' he said had chased him through the village. No one else had seen anything unusual so they were all putting it down to his imagination!

ON THE ROAD

Back in 1973 Mr and Mrs Hudd were convinced they were being haunted by a ghost car, ever since they had moved into the Lodge near Tiverton three years previously. The whole family would hear the roar of an engine along the drive, the double click of a car door closing and the creaking of a garden gate. Their pet dogs responded and several members of the family 'felt' a presence but despite efforts to find out who or what it was they never did. They were certain it was a friendly ghost and would have been quite happy to keep it around but Mr Hudd, who still lives in the house, says that in recent years their ghost appears to have left them alone.

Perhaps the ghost car was taken in to a garage for repairs... Mr Rogers from Paignton rang to tell me of a very unusual occurrence, a poltergeist in a garage. Spanners, screw drivers and even heavier objects flew about, the centre of the disturbance seeming to be an old Austin Seven, which had been involved in an accident. Spots of blood appeared on the wings and body, which disappeared again just as suddenly. He and all his friends linked arms and, making a solid line, walked right across the garage, so no one could have been playing games.

A FAVOURITE OLD HAUNT

Berry Pomeroy castle must be the most haunted castle in Devon and certainly much has been written about it and its hauntings. Chips Barber recalls playing there when he was a boy. With some friends, he was kicking a football around when it disappeared over the castle ramparts and rebounded down a flight of steps into Saint Margaret's Tower. He went to recover it from this gloomy dungeon-like chamber. As he stooped to pick it up he felt the presence of someone close by and turned in time to see the swirling of long skirts disappear up the steps, as if he'd been followed down. A little later, out in the light of day, the castle custodian approached them to say that the castle was now closing and asked them if there was anyone else around. Chips pointed out that he'd seen a lady in the tower but none of the others had seen anyone leave!

Still on the subject of Berry Pomeroy, I received a long and very interesting letter from Mr Upton of Paignton who said there are two incidents connected with this area that he finds very strange.

Firstly he was riding his motor bike along the lane beneath the area where the knights on horseback were said to have plunged to their death, when the machine suddenly, and for no apparent reason, went completely out of control, throwing him into a nearby ditch. Fortunately he was only badly shaken and not seriously hurt. There was nothing found to be wrong with the machine, the road was dry and he is an experienced rider.

Previously, when his wife was a young girl, she and her parents had visited the castle. Her mother had gone down into the cellars beneath the castle and become very frightened as she could not find her way out. At that moment a lady in white appeared and pointed out the way up the stairs. Her companions asked her to whom she had been talking, and she explained. On the way out they told the curator who gave them an odd look and said, "No one else has come inside and if it had been a member of the staff they would have been wearing a badge like mine."

AN ARMY OF GHOSTS

Ann lives at Slapton and takes in summer visitors and she related what happened to some visitors on 28 April one year...

It was still dark when the guest woke, but she felt dawn was near although no birds were singing. She thought she heard the sound of a storm coming from the sea as the window was open to the mild April night. She could also hear men's voices shouting.

She had to get up and in doing so disturbed her sister who was sharing the room, but Elaine said she had been awake for some time and also had heard sounds coming from the beach. They could hear gunfire and screams of men in pain. They both went to the window and opened it wider, but could see nothing. Then there was the sound of what could only be described as a battle of some kind out at sea. Gunfire and men's cries as if they came from some distance away. They were most surprised no one else in the house had been disturbed. Gradually the noises faded but of course they could not sleep.

At breakfast they asked their fellow guests and Ann if they had heard anything, but they hadn't. It was then Ann told them about the terrible battle that had taken place in the bay on 28 April 1943. Eight landing craft had been intercepted by nine German E boats, GST 507 was struck by a torpedo and caught fire, and the survivors abandoned ship. A few minutes later LST 531 was hit by two torpedoes, rolled over and sank. LST 289 opened fire on the E boats, which retaliated with a torpedo hit. Twelve men were killed but the landing craft managed to make Dartmouth harbour. The loss of life during this brief action was 197 sailors and 441 soldiers. Ann then showed them the full account in a book.

So just what did happen to those two sisters on holiday in the South Hams on that April morning? They had absolutely no previous knowledge even of the fact that the area had ever been evacuated or used by the USA troops and certainly not of any battle at sea. Again comes my theory that events fraught with powerful human emotions leave behind some kind of impression capable of being picked up by someone sufficiently sensitive. Did they tune in to some kind of psychic sound trace of the battle, which had brought death and destruction to all those men?

THE HITCHHIKING GHOST

Here I would like to go on to my friend Harry Unsworth of Newton Abbot who has given me so much wonderful material to mull over. He was the man who told me first about the Phantom Hitchhiker on the A38 and he has such an unusual sequel to the tale that it is definitely worth repeating here.

A section of this road has an evil reputation as the haunt of a phantom who, with a torch, tries to flag down passing motorists at night. This tradition had been well established for a number of years and in August 1970 a Mrs K. Swithenbank told the *Western Morning News* that while she was travelling from the village of Oake to Taunton, late one evening, she saw a middle-aged man in a long grey overcoat standing in the middle of the road near Heatherton Grange Hotel. He seemed to be holding a torch pointing to the ground and he appeared so suddenly round a bend that she had to brake violently. There was no impact and the road was completely empty in both directions.

Two other motorists and a motorcyclist had the same experience, the latter at White Ball four miles to the west. These reports in the press prompted Harry Unsworth, who at that time was a long distance lorry driver of Exeter, to break a twelve year silence and contact the newspaper himself with an experience he had kept quiet about, partly for fear of ridicule, but mainly because, being a practical and down-to-earth man, he could scarcely believe it himself.

He described how he had been driving back to his depot at Cullompton at about 3 am when he had been flagged down near the Blackbird Inn, one mile west of Heatherton Grange, by a man in a grey coat carrying a torch. It was a foul night and the man was hatless with hair hanging almost to his collar. Against his better judgement, and usual rule of not picking up random hitch hikers, Harry gave him a lift.

The man appeared, from his speech, to be well educated and asked to be dropped at the old Beam Bridge at Holcombe. All his conversation was of the terrible and gruesome accidents that had occurred at the Bridge, so Harry was not sorry to get rid of his passenger.

Several days later, again in the early hours of the morning, he was astonished to see the same person on the same spot in the same weather conditions.

There was a repeat performance of the former occasion.

To do it twice really seemed incredible, and yet a month later he was there again. The rain, the torch, the hour and the conversation were identical. Harry began to think he was dealing with someone mentally disturbed and was much relieved when, although he drove along the same place several times, he saw no more of the stranger. Until …

In November 1958 the man was back, and exactly the same sequence of events followed, but this time when they stopped at the bridge the man asked Harry if he would wait while he collected some cases as he wanted to go farther along the road.

Harry waited and waited, for twenty minutes, then he drove off.

Three miles ahead he saw a torch being waved frantically and, thinking it might be a motorist in trouble, he stopped. But when his headlights shone fully on the figure he saw to his horror it was the man in the grey coat with the wet, straggling hair. His own hair literally stood on end for no vehicle had passed him and it would have been quite impossible for the man to have covered the distance on foot. He was really alarmed and swerved to avoid the man. As he did so the man leapt in front of the lorry, Harry slammed on the brakes knowing he must have hit him. His articulated vehicle jackknifed but he managed to bring it under control. He got down and looked back. The figure still stood in the middle of the road shaking his fist and swearing. Then suddenly he turned and literally vanished into thin air.

Shaking from head to foot, and covered no doubt with goose pimples, Harry leapt back into his cab, straightened out the lorry and drove furiously to where something like normality existed. He told me he can only think that as so many motorists and pedestrians have died on this stretch, this must be some kind of manifestation and this poor figure is doomed to seek a lift from passing vehicles forever.

And now to the sequel. Harry rang me to remind me of this story and to say there was more, something he had never told anyone. After the report had appeared in the newspaper he had a visit from two 'pasty-faced teenagers with short blonde hair who looked like twins'. These two boys appeared to be students and Harry assumed they came from Exeter University. They had a very abrupt manner, and they asked him if he had noticed any particular smell about the passenger, what clothes he was wearing, the manner of his speech and – oddly – did he talk **to** Harry or **through** him.

They were very persistent in their quest for details but eventually, after about ten minutes, they thanked him for his time, and went down the steps towards the street. At the time Harry was living in a cul-de-sac with the turning point right outside his house and he noticed a white Mini parked in the turning bay, which he presumed was their vehicle. He had just closed the door, and hadn't even taken his hand off the handle, when he remembered a small incident he had overlooked. He reopened the door and the street was empty! The strange pair and the Mini had apparently vanished into thin air. The Avenue is at least a quarter of a mile long with no turnings so it would have been impossible in the time for that car to have turned and got out of sight!

BISHOP LACY

When researching for haunted pubs that don't have all their spirits on the optic, I investigated the Bishop Lacy at Chudleigh. This was the only building left standing whole after the terrible fire of 1807. In the fourteenth century Bishop Edmund Lacey chose Chudleigh for his summer vacation, staying at the monastery, parts of which can still be seen. The Inn was said to be haunted by a cloaked figure, which the then landlord told me he had seen at closing time. Taking it at first to be a lingering customer he pointed out that he was closing the bar. The man took no notice and started to go up the stairs. The landlord shouted after him and then followed him. He met his wife coming down and explained the position, but no one had passed her!

It seems either this chap returned with different ideas in mind, or a new spirit then took over. He walked out without paying, and also stole the teaspoons! This mad monk wandered along the corridors in brown robes. He also appeared at full moon and took a dislike to things modern such as heating and electricity. A later landlord, Steve Folds, had several encounters of a spirit kind with the ghost but, apart from the missing teaspoons, didn't find him harmful. It seems when the full moon was approaching, the TV lounge exuded a musty smell and became bitterly cold. At one time all the guests' digital watches started to flash and went back five minutes – it also gave the vacuum cleaner a kind of life of its own and was inclined to turn up the heating during the night, making Steve Folds remark that he had no objection to this, but would've liked a bit of cost-sharing towards the electricity bill!

THE NOT VERY CIVIL WAR GHOST

I read in the *Western Morning News* that the curse of Widey Lodge has reappeared. It seems that cracks had begun to appear in the outside lane of the A38 Manadon flyover at Plymouth making motorists curse when they found cones closing off the lane. Like many similar psychic phenomena, this particular curse seems to attack those who tamper with historic sites in the name of progress. Widey Lodge, which was the last remnant of Widey Court, an historic mansion once mentioned in the Domesday Book and later used as King Charles' headquarters during the Civil War, was demolished in 1983 to make way for the A38. Widey Court was long rumoured to be haunted with its priest holes, secret passages and tunnels, but all had remained quiet until the Lodge came down. Then workmen building the road discovered to their horror that they were dicing with death as an unexploded wartime bomb was disturbed, having been sliced into and trampled all over by the men before it was noticed. Then a mis-aimed excavator on the ill-fated road scheme put the entire telephone network out of action; one of the massive pits was mysteriously flooded; and fire broke out in the little village of the contractors' wooden huts.

The County Engineer dismissed all this as nothing, which could well have been tempting fate, and the ghost if it was listening!

HAUNTED BY A DREAM?

Now for something different. It is many years since I first met Vincent Wills from St Thomas in Exeter. We both wrote fiction for the same publishing house, and I was a visitor judging short stories at the Writer's Club to which he belonged. Sadly he has now died but I would like to relate the following fascinating story he told me, as a small tribute to his memory.

I had a relative who lived in the parish of Dunsford who claimed actually to have witnessed the bemused Squire Fulford driving the phantom coach with its four headless horses on this certain night of the year, and he often related the story with hair raising relish on winter evenings around the open hearth of the farmhouse where I used to spend my boyhood holidays.

I personally experienced something I have always regarded as a mild brush with the supernatural very closely associated with the Fulford mansion at Dunsford.

My father was born at Westland – one of the farms on the Fulford estate. It was a small farm and a poor one, so at the age of thirteen my father left home and went off to earn his living as a baker. Just after the end of the First World War we were living at Exmouth, my father was working at Exeter so I only saw him briefly weekends. My mother had some previous nursing experience and she augmented our precious income by doing some night nursing so, as an only child, I was frequently left in the house alone. My mother used to leave a night light burning on the dressing table, and I never had the slightest fear of being left alone because she was always there in the morning to give me my breakfast and get me off to school – until one night I awakened from a terrifying nightmare.

I was lost in the crumbling passageway of a rambling old country mansion. The wooden panelling along the lower portion of the walls was decaying with age; the colouring flaking off the plaster above. I groped my way along to the end of the passage, through a narrow doorway, to find myself in a large gloomy attic.

The attic was packed tight with children's toys – a rocking horse, a dolls' pram, a huge fort with lead soldiers arrayed round its turrets, and a myriad of other playthings. The size of them and the hideous conglomeration they created, frightened me.

At the far end of the attic I could see a narrow shaft of light. I stumbled hopefully towards it, keeping as far away as I could from the objects I somehow found so distasteful. Reaching it I found that the light came from under a large door. By lying flat on my stomach I was able to look into a vast empty room with a beautifully polished floor. Straining even further, I found myself looking upwards towards the source of light. It came from a brilliant crystal chandelier, in the centre of which was a large green pendant. I sprang to my feet and struggled desperately with the huge handle of the door, trying to wrench it open, but it wouldn't budge.

I woke up to see the shadow of the jug in the washbasin performing the most grotesque movements around the walls of my room as the night-light flickered on the point of going out.

Convinced that childhood's dreaded 'bogeyman' had arrived, the night-light spluttered feebly and went out.

I lay awake in the darkness, too petrified to move, knowing it was useless to scream out. The stupid dream recurred with frightening regularity through my childhood. During adolescence and for many years after I married, it persisted with irritating annoyance. Then quite suddenly it was wiped out by an astonishing sequel.

I was working in the office of a small plumbing and heating engineering firm at Exeter who had a contract at the start of every winter to clear away the leaves and broken branches from the roofs at Fulford House and repair any splits in the lead valleys and gutterings. In those days few workmen had a vehicle of their own; one of the bosses would take them to the site in the morning and fetch them home in the evening. On this particular afternoon an unexpected emergency made it necessary for me to drive out to Fulford House and bring the plumber home.

Arriving at the house, Mrs Fulford herself came to the door and told me she would have to take me to the plumber as he was working under the roof where a leak had been discovered in one of the huge lead lined water tanks.

We had to cross a small stone walled courtyard to get there, and the moment Mrs Fulford unlocked the round-topped, oaken door in the grey granite wall, I recognised the passage in which I had got lost in that frightening nightmare of my childhood. The panelling was old and crumbling, the distemper flaking off the walls about it. She took me along a maze of passages and up some flights of stairs until we reached the gabled loft under the roof. We

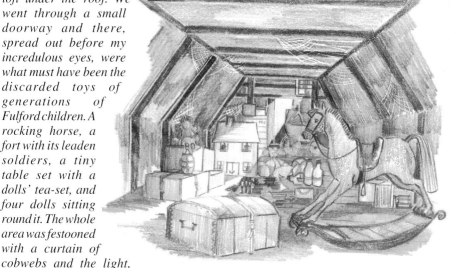

went through a small doorway and there, spread out before my incredulous eyes, were what must have been the discarded toys of generations of Fulford children. A rocking horse, a fort with its leaden soldiers, a tiny table set with a dolls' tea-set, and four dolls sitting round it. The whole area was festooned with a curtain of cobwebs and the light, shining through them from the skylight above, gave everything a ghostly, eerie appearance.

The workman, surprised to see a member of the office staff, was picking up his tools in readiness to leave, and as I turned to return the way I had come he said to me, "Hang on a *minute, let's go down this way. There's something I'd like to show you whilst you're here."*

He led me down another stairway that joined the main staircase of the mansion. He opened a door leading off the hall, and the first thing that met my gaze was the beautifully polished floor of the ballroom.

"The Colonel's just had that put in," the workman told me, "Don't you think it's beautiful?"

I agreed and my gaze automatically strayed in the direction of the decorated ceiling. And there, suspended from its centre, was one of the loveliest crystal chandeliers I have ever seen. The flick of a switch brought it cascading to brilliance and life. Its centre piece thrust back at me a gleaming, emerald challenge.

I was never bothered with the dream afterwards.

I have always believed that happenings of this nature are bound to have some perfectly logical explanation, and curious to unravel the mystery of this one, I remember asking my cousins at Burnwell, the farmhouse in the same parish where I used to spend my school holidays – if I could have lost myself there as a child, perhaps at a summer fete or some such social occasion, to be told it was extremely unlikely. Fulford House was a long way from the village of Dunsford, and too isolated for it ever to have been used for a function of this sort.

When I mentioned this story on the radio, a man rang me afterwards to ask me if I knew that there had been a murder in that attic. Unfortunately he then rang off.

I found this story very similar to the one of Joan and her dream of the millhouse in my book *Tales of the Unexplained in Devon* which could have been a form of déjà vu through hereditary genes.

I REMEMBER WHEN?

Here is a story which must be of 'inherited memory' as there seems to be no other explanation. Sent by Joan Amos of Peter Tavy, I feel she has given it a very apt title.

Ever since I was a child I have had a gift of psychic happening, this can be in the form of precognition dreams, or flash visions, which I don't always understand until some later date, when it connects up with some future happening. I have a theory that this is due to my ancestry as on my mother's side my folks were Cornish seafaring people, my grandfather being a well known Merchant Navy Captain with his own three-masted schooner.

On my father's side the family goes back to the fifteenth century as farming folk in a village high on Dartmoor from whence came the family name – Hexworthy, so both sides lived close to nature.

As my Dad died at an early age, when I was only four years old, my mother was left to bring up three little children, and arrangements were made that I, as the eldest, should live with my grandma and grandfather. I was with them until he had a stroke and died. I tell you all this to explain why I was so fond of my grandparents and felt so close to them.

Years passed until, as an adult with children of my own, I took a trip into the countryside near Plymouth to have a day out at a fancy dress show. Arriving by bus at Cornwood with a friend and the children, we discovered we had to enter through some lodge gates, and go down a long gravel drive to reach the mansion where the fancy dress fête was to be held.

I began to get a peculiar eerie feeling as we walked down the drive, I particularly remember the overhead canopy of leaves with the shafts of sunlight piercing through and although it was a hot day I felt chilled right through my body and I was trembling all over. I could hear running water from a stream. At last we reached the end of the drive where the trees ended and opened out to green lawns and a large manor house. Workmen on ladders were painting the front windows. On enquiring we found that we had got the date wrong and the fête wasn't until the following week but we were told there was a sports day at the next village. This was several miles distant so I went to the front door to ask if there was a bus service. I was greeted by an extremely nice elderly gentleman whom I discovered later was a retired Admiral.

He invited me into a large parlour while he went to the telephone to find out the bus times. Alone in the room I began to look around. It was a very hot day and I was glad to be in the cool. The room was full of antique furniture, polished wood, and a big deep sofa with old fashioned chintz covers. But the thing that attracted my attention most was the french windows with long velvet curtains overlooking a green lawn with a sundial in the centre.

As I stood looking at this view I began to feel a cold and prickly sensation, everything became cloudy – I felt as if the present had faded away and I was in another age. That view was so familiar to me – I knew it so well, and I had been in the room before – and yet how could I? I had never been in this area before.

The man returned, breaking the spell. He looked at me and asked if I was feeling all right. I said I felt a little faint. He fetched me a glass of water and, as I turned again towards the window, once more the feeling of familiarity returned stronger than ever and I knew I had stood in that room before and looked at that lawn many times. I began to shiver uncontrollably and was glad when my glass of water arrived and seemed to return me to normality – and so we went on our way, but I could not shake off that feeling of 'belonging' in that house.

Years passed but I still recalled it constantly. Twenty-five years later I think I discovered the answer. I went to tea with an old aunt in her eighties. The table was laid in Edwardian fashion. When we had finished tea the conversation turned to family history – the one thing we had in common. So I asked a question which had often puzzled me. I wanted to know how grandma and grandad met for I knew transport had been difficult in those days, and people didn't travel around. Grandma came from a little village near Exeter and was known as the Belle of Trusham, whereas grandad was born in a village near Tavistock called Lamerton.

My aunt told me how Grandma, as a young woman, went into service and took a position as a nanny with the Rolls family, her charge being the young Charles Rolls who later produced the Rolls Royce engine. However her work took her far away to Wales. She wasn't happy there and applied for a job as parlour maid at a large country house back in her native Devon. Meanwhile my grandad had served his apprenticeship as a stable boy and graduated to a position as groom at the same manor house. One day he was told to take the pony and trap to the nearest railway station to pick up the new parlourmaid. He picked up her belongings and took her back where she settled into her job and romance blossomed between them. Eventually a marriage was arranged and the family for whom they worked were very fond of the couple, so when the big day came a reception was held for them up at the Big House.

At this point of the story I jumped to my feet shouting "Stop, stop, don't tell me any more – I KNOW – it was Delamore House."

My aunt looked at me in amazement and said, "My dear Joan, how ever did you know that?" I told her of my experience twenty-five years earlier. Now I knew why I felt what I did when I walked into that parlour, which my grandmother had tended with loving care because she was so happy. I wonder now how many times she must have looked, dreamily, out of those french windows until the view was imprinted on her memory and eventually on mine.

So, did I go back in time that day? Was I standing in the same place that my grandmother had stood? Or was I then part of her remembering? Something very strange happened to me that day – unexplainable as I knew nothing about this story nor had I ever been in that house before in my life.

THE COTTAGE THAT NEVER WAS

Now a letter I received from Derrick Warren, who at one time lived in Torquay. He wrote: *In October 1955 I was revising the l:25000 Ordnance Survey maps in the Haytor area. Sitting on a hillside below Haytor village overlooking the countryside down to Bovey Tracey and with the old plans spread out on the grass, I was assessing and ordering my next few days' work, i.e. checking to see what new buildings or fences there were to be surveyed, what hedges had been removed and to list certain houses, the names of which I had to collect.*

In a very wooded and underdeveloped area about a mile away I saw a cottage which did not appear on the old map and, as it was obviously occupied, clothes were blowing on the line and smoke coming from the chimney, I noted that I would have to walk up the lane on which it was situated (this was on the map) in order to survey it and collect its name. When, in a couple of days, my work reached that area, I was unable to find it and come to the conclusion that I had made a mistake as to its location and thought no more of it.

Some two weeks later, I was working in Brimley and the lady whose house I was surveying, invited me in for coffee. During our conversation she asked me if I had an old map of the area as she was trying to find out about a cottage she had seen but had subsequently been unable to find. It transpired that a year previously, on first coming to live in the village, she had taken her dog for a walk over the hills and, looking back to between Bovey and Brimley had seen a cottage, obviously lived in as she put it, near an old lane. Thinking this would make a nice walk, she later traced the lane but could not see any cottage. Her curiosity aroused, she had tried in vain to find out from local characters and the District Council if there was any record of a cottage ever having been there. I then told her of my sighting and, to our amazement, our descriptions tallied, and we were able to pin point its location.

I revisited the lane and surrounding fields, but could find no visible remains. However, roughly where we thought the cottage had been, the lane

hedge was comprised largely of myrtle, a hedging plant much favoured by old country people for a garden hedge, as it is evergreen and not eaten by cattle or sheep.

I left the area in 1956 and was living in Chard when my sister excitedly brought me a book she had borrowed from the library Folklore and Magic of Dartmoor by Ruth St Leger-Gordon. One mystery quoted was the sighting by three separate people of a cottage which, on later investigation, did not exist. No exact location was given in the book beyond the fact that it was on the southern slopes of Dartmoor, as my two sightings had been.

A few months later I was moved to Torquay and in 1966 some work took me to Sticklepath where Mrs St Leger-Gordon lived. I visited her and told her my story, but she asked me immediately not to reveal my location of the cottage. She called in a neighbour to act as an independent witness and we both marked our one inch maps with our respective locations and gave them to him. He confirmed they were identical.

Ruth St leger-Gordon had already written an account in her book The Witchcraft and Folklore of Dartmoor which I had quoted over the air saying that many houses, from cottage to mansion, have their recognised ghosts and sometimes a house itself seems to figure as a phantom. As a result, I had several letters and phone calls on this subject.

One call was from Norma, who asked me if I had ever heard of a house 'hating' a person. Some time ago she and her husband had been house hunting and they found the perfect house, but directly she entered it she knew it hated and rejected her; the atmosphere was terrible. No one else felt it, but she said they didn't buy it because she could never have lived in it. The people who did buy it have lived there for years and been perfectly okay – so are we back to déjà vu, had perhaps some of Norma's ancestors either lived there, or visited, and something terrible had happened, filling her with this dread. Who knows?

HOMESICK GHOSTS?

'Ronnie' rang to tell me how her husband was a complete sceptic over ghosts but they bought an old property in the West Country that was said to be haunted by an elderly woman, at which information her husband fell about laughing.

While he was doing some repairs and alterations he kept seeing this old woman hanging about dressed in old fashioned clothes. He thought it odd but imagined she was some old villager who was nosy. However the neighbours brought up the question of the old lady who had once lived there and was said to haunt the house – he confessed what he had seen but said he was not in the least afraid, it was obvious the woman had become very attached to the house and came to see what he was doing in the way of alterations. The house had always had a lovely warm feeling about it and a welcoming atmosphere, and when Ronnie's husband finally put down a Tarmac drive, the ghost never reappeared. Apparently she was quite satisfied with what had been done!

Muriel from Newton Abbot sent me her story of what happened when she and her husband had been left a small legacy with which they decided to buy a cottage in the country.

They spent some time exploring and found just what they fancied on the corner of a country lane. It was empty with a "For Sale" board outside, which looked as if it had been there some time. They parked the car at the top of a hill overlooking the cottage and walked back down the hill to have a look around. There was a pathway that looked as though the farmer used it to get to his fields. The cottage gate opened from this. There was a small garden with a wall on two sides and high hedges on the others. Quite naturally the doors of the cottage were locked so they peered through the windows and saw that a good deal of work needed doing.

Walking back to the car they looked back at the cottage and saw a lady dressed in dark brown robes, rather like a nun, walking down the side pathway and into the gate to the cottage. They dashed back thinking perhaps she had a key and they would be able to look around. But when they reached the cottage there was no sign of the lady, the gate was closed and the garden had no other outlet. She had simply disappeared. Not too surprisingly they decided not to buy but often wonder if it is now occupied and whether the occupants share it with the strange lady dressed in brown.

Mary from Stockleigh Pomeroy also tells of an old lady, this time in a house at Thorverton. Three cottages had been knocked into one and Mary, who moved into it in 1966, knew that some of the building dated back to 1680.

Whenever she was cleaning or hoovering she was aware of someone watching in the doorway – just watching – she was small and dressed in black with a white apron, her hair swept back, hands clasped in front. A very benign lady and always very still. Sometimes Mary's mother felt she was being tapped on the shoulder, and would say, "I hope the old devil gives me some peace tonight."

One day some visitors came to look at the garden and the lady said she had been born in the house – Hannabusses – and pointed to a window, "My grandmother's room, old Mrs Matthews' granddaughter." She described her and the appearance tallied exactly. She went on, "She was a lovely old lady but very deaf and used to stand and appear to be listening. If she wanted to speak she would tap hard on one's shoulder". Mary's small grandson slept in the room and had to be moved, saying he didn't like the lady who stood by his bed, listening.

Kitty and George from Newton Abbot wrote to me about a large Victorian house in which they had lived in Newton Abbot. It was over 100 years old with huge high rooms, black marble fireplaces etc. Kitty was doing the housework one day when her husband was out shopping. Going down the stairs she saw a figure, which she thought was her husband, in the vestibule with his back towards her. He was wearing a grey raincoat and carrying a basket. She shouted, "Oh George, I'm glad you're back," and went on into the dining room. She went on chatting to him and then went back into the hall, which was empty. She realised then that she had seen an apparition for her husband didn't own a grey raincoat and had no such basket either. There was no one else in the house at the time. Somehow the house always had the 'beyond the grave' feeling although they were never actually frightened but they were not sorry to leave it.

A lady from Brampford Speke, who wished to remain anonymous, wrote me a long and very interesting letter about peculiar noises in her house which became apparent after she had been listening to my talk on the radio, particularly about the fact that sometimes it seemed talking of such things activated them!

During a time they lived in Tiverton she, and many other people who stayed with her, felt very uncomfortable in one particular bedroom and, as a child, she had encountered "a man in black" on the stairs of her aunt's house. Also things got misplaced to reappear almost immediately somewhere else. One night she woke up fighting for breath to find the sheet on her bed was being stuffed into her mouth and she had to put up a great struggle to get free. She finished, "Since then I have read that things called poltergeists can be activated in households where there is mental or emotional stress and as both my mother and I were going through difficult times I wonder if this is the explanation."

Marian from Exeter wrote about her twenty-year-old daughter who had joined the army three years before and, after her initial training, had been posted to Shoeburyness near Southend. She was quartered in conventional barracks and one night, just as she was going off to sleep, with her head under the clothes, a childhood habit, she was suddenly aware of the sound of breathing close to her. At first she thought it was her room mate, but then she heard her cough from the other side of the room. The breathing moved closer until within a few inches of her head, making her very frightened. Eventually she fetched her commanding officer, who tried to calm her. She was white and shaking. Several of the girls had heard knockings and it had been proved the corridor was haunted. In the two years she was there she had more encounters of this kind. It seems there had been a bad fire in the building at one time in which people had died. After the place was rebuilt and soldiers billeted there, they were so disturbed that they refused to sleep there and it was then it was made over to the Women's Royal Army Corps.

A SIXTH SENSE?

Alan wrote from Exmouth to tell me the following story. He says he has had many similar experiences to the one here but tries to suppress them. This particular one started one Thursday at 10 am. He could smell petrol very strongly and asked David in the shop if he could smell it too. He said he couldn't but Alan still suggested that David be very careful when he went to the cash and carry in Exeter. The smell persisted all day and he felt very nervous, as a petrol station kept springing to mind. On Friday the smell stopped. On Saturday afternoon the phone rang at 5.30. Alan's sister, who lives in a mining village called Arley near Coventry, had gone to shop at the hypermarket but, before they reached it, David who was driving, pulled in for petrol. As he did so a car hit him and then four more piled up behind. His sister had a broken collar bone and broken glass in her face, her husband was also cut and so were the others. It is strange he should receive this form of warning the day before.

Phyllis from Dunsford wrote enclosing some fascinating snippets. The first thing she mentioned was a dream she had many years ago about a funeral. She didn't know whose it was and was terribly upset and crying. Wondering whether it might be her mum or dad kept her mind constantly returning to it. It was only a week or so later that she was at a whist drive with her mum when they heard her uncle, who had lodged with her mum and dad, had died suddenly of a heart attack. Did she have a premonition of his death?

On another occasion, more recently, Phyllis was Christmas shopping and realised, when she arrived home, she had left some tobacco in the shop. Several times she kept hearing the words "Stop him, Stop him!" without knowing what it meant. She wondered if someone had been shop lifting and just how she would react under such circumstances. Next time she went into town she parked her car outside the shop where she had bought and left the tobacco. She had just got out of the car when a young lad came running down the road carrying something in his hand. A man was running after calling, "Stop him, stop him!" but the thief got away.

And finally, Bruce was their 'indoor dog', a cross between a whippet and an Alsatian, but very gentle. When they went out they always let him have the run of the bungalow, and although they didn't approve, he loved to go and curl up on their bed. As time passed he gradually became deaf and he didn't hear them come in so they would find him still curled up on the bed. As always happens in old age, they had to have him put to sleep as he started to fall over and they didn't like to see that. Several times after that when Phyllis had gone to bed and been asleep she woke up and found she couldn't move her legs as there seemed to be a heavy weight on them. She kept calm and drifted off to sleep again. A couple of times her daughter asked if gran's dog had been down in her room during the night. The answer was always "no" as he was shut up in the kitchen. So was it Bruce who came back to visit them for a while?

Pauline from Paignton related a strange experience she and her husband had before they came to live in Devon – none the less interesting for that. She said that one night, before they were married, her husband-to-be was seeing her home and they were walking down Bloemfontein Road in Shepherd's Bush when they saw a lorry travelling at speed towards them. As they approached a T-Junction at South Africa Road, also travelling at speed coming towards the junction, along South Africa Road, was a cyclist so there was no possible way they could avoid each other. Pauline stopped in her tracks and held her hands to her face. The lorry carried on its sweet way and the cyclist vanished into thin air. They spent half an hour searching for him to no avail. But a few days later, in the local paper, it was reported that a lorry had collided with a cyclist who was killed two days after they had witnessed it!

I appealed for material for this book on local radio and, just before I came off the air, after a broadcast in March 1987, a lady rang who was obviously very distressed and did not wish to give her name. She said that a few days earlier she had been walking along the beach at Broadsands with her children when she had an overwhelming feeling that there was a dead body nearby. Not wanting her children to see such a thing, she immediately decided to leave the beach. Within a few days she read in the paper that a dead body had indeed been found within a few yards of where she had experienced the feeling.

THOU SHALT NOT TRESPASS

Helen from Dawlish sent me a press cutting, on yellowing, fragile paper, of the "Bartons Ghost" – written by Henry Knight who died in London in 1935.

Many years ago where Barton Villas now stand there stood a large old fashioned house surrounded by several acres of land beside an extensive orchard. At the time of my story the house was empty, it was going to be pulled down and the land sold for building. I happened to be in Dawlish on Christmas Eve as a visitor and it entered my boyish head that a peep at Barton House would be a daring feat to accomplish at night.

The ground was thickly covered with snow, the moon shining brightly through the trees. I crept up Barton Lane and reached the tall palings guarding the orchard, scaled them and dropped over. The windows of the house were dark and desolate, the roof covered with snow. I pushed open the massive oaken door and entered the hall. A broad oak staircase led to the upper floor. I ascended the steps, and selecting a door opened it and entered. The door swung to behind me making my heart beat rapidly. Then I heard the front door creak on its hinges and though I heard no footsteps an indescribable sensation told me someone was ascending the staircase. I opened the bedroom door and, to my horror, saw the form of a man in a monk's garb standing at the top of the staircase. In the brilliant moonlight I could distinctly see the moulding of the wainscot on the other side of the gallery through his body.

I was rooted to the spot, my hair standing on end. How long I stood spell bound I cannot say, it seemed ages but was probably a few seconds. Suddenly, with a long drawn out sigh, the apparition vanished through a door directly opposite where I stood. Immediately afterwards I was horrified to hear a blood curdling shriek of pain followed by a thud as of some heavy body falling to the ground, while from under the door slowly trickled a stream of blood. I sank to the ground in a swoon.

On recovering my senses the moon was still shining brightly. With a shudder I looked towards the door through which my ghostly visitor had vanished, fondly hoping that what I had gone through was a nightmare brought on by a disordered imagination.

No! For horror of horrors there was the stream of bright red blood now formed into a ghastly pool; while from within came deep groans as of one in the agonies of death, followed by a burst of fiendish laughter.

I waited to hear no more, as fast as my tottering steps would take me I ran down the stairs, opened the door, and fled across the orchard, gained the palings, scaled them and hurried home.

The old house was razed to the ground soon after my boyish escapade, and later the present villas were erected. But the events of that night will never be effaced from my memory. That some dreadful deed was done there, perhaps in the dim dark ages of long ago I have no manner of doubt, and that what I saw was a reality, and no dream – there can be no question.

Helen also sent a photograph of a house "Barton Garth" which she says was built in 1880 and stands in a small part of the orchard which then belonged to Barton House. She was born in this house, which was occupied by her family (Cornelius) from 1897 to 1979 when it was sold. Sometime during 1969 she too saw a ghost, but whether it was the same one from Barton House we shall never know.

THE GHOST OF CHRISTMAS PRESENT

The next story, which is most incredibly fascinating, is also one which appeared first in the press, in the *Mid Devon Advertiser* on Christmas Eve 1986. It was sent to me by the author, John Abelard of East Ogwell (a pen name), and he has kindly given me full permission to reproduce it.

A curious event occurred last Christmas in our family circle, which I should like to share with your readers.

It began in fact two years ago, on Christmas Day, as we sat round the dinner table musing on past times and on the dear friends and relations who had made their final exits into the other world.

As often happens on these occasions, the conversation had drifted into a sombre discussion of life after death, a topic most unsuitable for a jolly Christmas dinner!

In an attempt to inject a note of gaiety into the proceedings, my father proposed a toast, and promised that when he died he would somehow get in touch with us.

There was a rock-crystal ashtray on my father's knee in which a fat Cuban cigar slowly smouldered.

"You see this ashtray?" my father asked, "Well, when I die I'll come back and smash it. Just to prove I've finally given up smoking!"

We laughed and the matter was soon forgotten as the plum pudding was carried in, all lit up in its dish of blazing brandy.

My father died within a month of making that last joke.

It had been noted at the time of his passing that my father's Swiss watch, an antique Audemars Piguet, had stopped at the moment of his death, as many old watches tend to do on the demise of their owners.

This watch had been placed on the mantelpiece inside the rock-crystal ashtray and there it had lain as a memento for the past year, perpetually frozen at 12.44.

It was last Christmas then, a full year after my father's death, that we all got together again.

It was late evening and twelve of us were sitting round the fire roasting chestnuts and drinking sherry. My mother rose to fetch the ashtray from the mantelpiece. As she crossed the room there was a high pitched vibration, like the sound of a tuning fork, and the rock crystal ashtray suddenly cracked into two symmetrical halves.

Had matters stopped there we should doubtless have found some plausible explanation for the splitting ashtray. But what happened next was so bizarre that I doubt if any rational explanation can be found for it.

Rooted to the spot, my mother was staring fixedly – not at the ashtray, but at the watch that lay cradled within the ashtray's newly formed fissure – the second hand of the watch had jerked into spasmodic life and was racing round the watch face.

My mother wordlessly held the watch out for us to see. The revolution of the little red hand was unmistakable. It was swishing round quite definitely at several times its ordinary speed. When the watch finally hiccupped to a halt at 12.50 (six minutes on the watch face) we couldn't help noting that in a actual fact only a minute had passed. During the minute out of time I personally neither saw nor sensed anything unusual, apart from the strange behaviour of the watch.

But my mother, my aunt and a nine-year-old niece all claim to have seen my father – standing in front of the fire, his dark eyes agleam, he was smoking a long cigar from which golden yellow streamers of smoke danced like ribbons of sunlight.

My mother looks like a young girl nowadays, quite radiant, as if she had tasted the honeydew of paradise.

PREMONITIONS IN TIMES OF TROUBLE

I'd like to mention crisis apparitions, sometimes called astral travelling, because I have had dozens of examples of these sent to me, even Peter Sellers told how he had found himself floating above his own body and looking down on it while he was being operated on – and he could actually tell the doctor and nurse what they had been talking about while he was unconscious. Could be very embarrassing as well as spooky!

Is it possible too that people can transmit an image of themselves many miles from their physical body? For instance the example of Chay Blyth's wife who had the terrible feeling of his being in acute danger so badly that she couldn't even eat her food and told her companion that she was sure something terrible had happened to her husband. Later it was proved that at that precise moment he had been rounding Cape Horn, his vessel had capsized and he was fighting for his life in the water.

There were hundreds of such occurrences reported during both the last World Wars – in the 1914/18 war over 400 a month – men in the forces undergoing terrible experiences and unconsciously transmitting an image of themselves to someone near and dear.

During a talk I gave in Exeter, Edna told me of her own experience during the last war. Her husband was a Spitfire pilot. One evening, as she sat by the fire in their cottage while he was on duty, she suddenly saw him sitting opposite her, badly injured down the right side with burns on his face and arm. She was shocked and stunned, sure it was a premonition of his death. But within hours he rang up to say he had been shot down in a dog fight over Kent but was okay, and he would be with her very shortly. He had been trapped in his crashed plane, which was on fire, but somehow he had managed to get free, all he had was a bad burn on his arm and face.

The following story was sent to Obelisk Publications by Vincent Wills shortly before his sad death, and as it is so beautifully written and fits so well into the context of this book, Mrs Wills kindly agreed to it being published in full here.

During the Second World War, labour in the baking trade became increasingly difficult to find. At one of the smaller bakeries in Exeter where I worked, we were often unable to find even casual labour in the trade.

When Fearis' bakery premises were adjoining The Bude, Paris Street, before they were destroyed in one of the blitzes on the city, my cousin Ronald, who was bakery manager there, had an apprentice awaiting call-up in the Royal Navy, who had expressed his willingness to come and work for us, if only for a few weeks, to help us over a particularly busy holiday period.

At 18, he was already a six-footer, sturdily built – an extremely, likable fellow with a mass of copper-coloured freckles and a spontaneously hearty laugh.

His workmates had nicknamed him Ski because of a comical mannerism he had adopted – prevalent during our wartime association with the Soviet Union – when people frequently ended their sentences with this three letter termination. He would greet you with, "Helloski! How are you todayski?" Then he would take leave of you with, "Cheerioski! See you tomorrowski!"

He had worked for us for nine weeks when he received his call-up papers. He left in high spirits, expressing his determination to make the Navy his career when hostilities were over. He underwent six weeks' shore training and was then posted to convoy duty in the English Channel.

A few weeks later his boat was torpedoed and he was reported missing. After an agonising period of uncertainty, his relatives were informed by the Admiralty that he must be presumed dead.

My father, who had also been engaged in the baking trade in Cornwall, had now reached retirement age and came to live with us at Exeter.

Ron and his family and ourselves lived in adjacent streets that ran parallel with one another in the southern part of the city. Our back gardens came out into a lane almost opposite each other, which gave easy access from one house to another, even during the hours of blackout.

It was a gloomy afternoon in late November. My father and I were snoozing in the firelight, on either side of the living room fire. At work it had been a particularly busy weekend with staff away sick, and I had slept soundly.

I wakened to see the living room door open, and a moment later, Ski's tall figure in naval greatcoat, respirator slung casually over his shoulder, the three letters HMS vividly imprinted on the hatband, framed in the doorway.

"Ski!" I burst out jubilantly.

I leapt from my chair, hand outstretched, and rushed to greet him, overjoyed to realise that he was alive and well.

He walked straight through me. At least, that was the uncanny feeling that I experienced.

I followed him out of the living room, through the kitchen, down three steps into the garden, across the lane, and saw him disappear through the back doorway of our cousin's house, illuminated by a soft light from the kitchen.

In the living room, Ron was busily engaged helping their young evacuee boy build a balsawood plane from a model construction kit. He looked up with surprise at my entrance and laughingly enquired what could have brought me there at that unusual hour of the day.

I told him I had come to see Ski.

"Ski!" His eyebrows puckered deeply with further surprise as he repeated the name after me. "But surely, you knew Ski was dead? He was killed more than a year ago – on convoy duty in the Channel."

"So everyone seems to believe. But I've just followed him here from our place."

He stared at me blankly, adhesive spilling from the tube he was holding, then his features relaxed and he burst into laughter.

"I don't know what sort of a bottle you've been getting yours out of, old man, but it must be a darn sight stronger than the stuff I've been getting out of mine!"

My eyes searched restlessly for some shred of evidence that the young Serviceman I was positive I had followed to my cousin's house, existed. I could find none. Reason prevailed; reluctantly I accepted the fact that I had indeed slept soundly and dreamt the whole thing.

The little boy was clamouring impatiently to finish his model Hurricane fighter, anxious to be allowed to apply the camouflage and RAF insignia to its fuselage and wings himself. Unable to conceal his amusement, Ron laughingly implored me to "keep off the bottle" as I left.

At home again, the flames of the newly built-up fire danced a warm welcome. The kettle was singing on its trivet. My father had prepared and laid tea in readiness for my wife's homecoming from her afternoon wartime job.

My father had never known Ski or anything about the tragedy concerning the uncertainty of his death. It had all happened before he came to live with us.

Sitting in his easy chair, a scone pierced onto the end of a toasting fork, he said to me, "Who was that young sailor who went through here earlier on?"

Spooky, to say the least!

A similar story came from Mary of Bishops Hull, telling of when her sister-in-law's brother was ill with cancer, and eventually he had to go into hospital. One evening her sister-in-law came home from work and her fifteen-year-old son Brian said his uncle had come in the door with him and gone upstairs to the bathroom. Mary's sister-in-law said, "Whatever are you saying, you know your Uncle Fred is in hospital and very ill." He replied, "Mum he came in the door with me, please go upstairs and see for yourself." Half an hour later another relative arrived to say Fred had passed away. Brian is married now but he will never forget this incredible incident and, knowing him, Mary is absolutely convinced he saw his uncle walk up the stairs.

Another similar tale was told to me by a member of a Women's Institute from the Plymouth area, but is actually confirmation of the same story that I have heard elsewhere.

In 1880 Helen Alexander, who was the Scottish maid of Lady Helen Waldgrave, fell ill on arriving at Antony House at Torpoint. The doctor diagnosed typhoid and one of the house maids was told to look after her as there was no qualified nurse available. One cold morning, when the maid was preparing some medicine for Helen, a stout, elderly woman dressed in red flannel night clothes and carrying a candle burst into the bedroom and, ignoring the maid, went over to the bedside. The maid immediately imagined someone had sent for Helen's mother, but as she went over to the bed to give the patient the medicine, she realised the elderly woman had vanished.

Helen died a few hours later. Her mother was sent for from Scotland for the funeral. The maid was astonished to see it was the same woman who had come into the bedroom that cold morning. It was discovered that Helen's mother wore exactly similar nightclothes to those the maid had seen even including a rent in the skirt, and an identical candlestick to the one she had been carrying, stood beside her bed in Scotland. It seems that Helen had not written to tell her family of her illness as she did not want to worry them, but her mother said that, shortly before the actual time of her daughter's death, she had experienced an overwhelming feeling of impending disaster.

GHOST TOAST!

Some people were kind enough to send in several experiences, such as the letter from Ann of Dawlish who tells me she has seen ghosts since the age of six. She came to live in Dartmouth in 1965 with her first husband, in a bungalow on the Churchfields Estate, Townstal, a pleasant sunny place with no bad atmosphere, but often she would smell burning toast and rush into the kitchen to see if her husband had left some under the grill. He never had.

Once she was sitting writing in the window and she glanced over at the hearth. She saw the figure of a tall man with a shock of grey hair standing on the rug before the fire. He seemed to be a pale mauve colour, but only the top half was visible. It was daylight but there was still a brilliant white aura round him, dazzling to see. For three days after there was an icy cold patch of air where he had been standing, and her cat refused to sit on the rug for days. When she told her neighbour about this the neighbour was amazed and said the description given was exactly that of the former owner's father, who was exceedingly fond of the bungalow.

They moved to Dawlish in 1971, and on a couple of occasions she has been to Berry Pomeroy castle, and once was just entering one of the towers with a friend when they were transfixed and seized with a dreadful feeling of terror. They fled as fast as they could into the sun.

One evening she saw a ghost at Longlands in Dawlish, it was dusk, she wore a tight fitting bodice and long skirt all in beige, quite opaque, but the horrifying part was she had no head – just a frilly collar – no neck or head!

At one time Ann worked in the food bar at the Mount Pleasant Inn, Dawlish Warren and had some experiences there of a poltergeist. Quite often jars of pickles and salad cream would be hurled from a shelf in the food display cabinet. A bunch of keys lifted themselves off a hook to be flung on the floor. She heard a dragging sound and saw a broken carved wood mirror frame slowly sliding along the floor. There was an odd atmosphere about the pub, perhaps because it has many associations with smugglers – signal lanterns were flashed from the window to luggers waiting offshore.

At another time she worked as a cook at Sefton Hall Convalescent Home in Dawlish, which was eventually closed in 1986. Numerous reports of odd sightings have occurred here. The building is made up of two old early nineteenth century houses joined together "Lanherne" and "Sefton". There is a very creepy atmosphere in the lower basement rooms and workmen have been known to refuse to work down there, and the laundry area is specially eerie. A blue lady has been seen in the kitchen and several people have seen a grey/blue figure around the building. One evening Ann saw a strange misty grey swirling shape by the kitchen tea urn and very often felt a malevolent presence watching her, especially near the food store.

Not far from Sefton Hall stands the Shaftesbury Theatre, and this is haunted by Esmeralda, who does strange things making lights come on and off. Once the cast arrived for a play to find every light on in the building although they had all been turned off before they went home.

A friend of Ann's was motoring past Powderham church one night with a friend, when they had a terrifying encounter with a white lady, and neither will ever go past that way at night any more.

PREMONITIONS

Mr Walker wrote from Upton Pyne, saying that most of his experiences can be checked.

He's had many dreams that have come true. On one occasion he had a dream of a plane crash and he made a drawing of the incident. He drew a picture of the plane and said eighty-three people died. He also heard a voice say, "Is the Pilot dead?" Another voice said, "He is dying". The next day a plane crashed with eighty-three dead. The pilot had lived for two hours.

On another occasion he saw a building on fire over water – people were running from it actually on fire. He drew the picture twenty-four hours before the event and gave a copy to his friends. At work next day his picture was identical; a big holiday complex with masses of plastic had caught fire and burning plastic had dropped on holidaymakers in the Isle of Man.

Mr Walker says that time and time again he makes statements to his wife, right out of the blue, with confidence and without thinking, and many come true. The only thing he cannot do is to pinpoint the accidents in advance.

Joan (not her real name) who now lives in Exeter, recalled the time when she lived in an old house at Cullompton; her husband was upstairs and she was sewing in the kitchen in a recess under the stairs. It was May, and the house was quiet but she suddenly heard a strange, cackling laughter. She mentioned it to her husband but it hadn't been him. One week later Joan's father died. The following year, again in May, Joan's husband heard

Haunted Happenings in Devon

a strange, cackling laughter and called her to come and listen. It was the same sound. One week later, his uncle died. Joan found out later that the sound she heard could well have been Death-watch beetles, which mate in May, but an old superstition says that you only hear them if someone is going to die. She is happy to accept that it was the beetles she heard … but no trace of their activity could be found!

A few years ago, Marilyn and her husband were deciding what to buy his mother for Christmas and they decided a torch would be good idea because, like many old people, if there was a power cut, she would use a candle, and at her age that was not a good thing.

A week later the whole family gathered in Mother's living room and everyone, except Mother, could clearly smell a candle burning. The smell was so strong that one of her sons went upstairs to find it, but there was no candle. The following week she died. It was after the funeral, when everyone was gathered together again, they all recalled how, in the week before their Father had died, everyone had clearly smelt his tobacco smoke – except him!

MEDIA ATTENTION?

But not all stories are about the past – some people think there are no new ghosts but when Pebble Mill TV studios opened in Birmingham in November 1971 there had been a fatal accident with one of the brickies during the building and in 1977, when rehearsing for a play, the producer, Michael Role and members of the cast, heard very odd noises and then actually saw an image of the man.

Whether or not ghosts are particularly attracted to the media is not known but certainly at the independent radio station, Plymouth Sound, sited in the shell of an old chapel, was the ghost of a little old lady, whilst at the Television South West studios, built on a Napoleonic Wars graveyard, at Derry's Cross Plymouth, all sorts of rumblings and strange occurrences took place. The ground floor of TSW's studio was particularly prone with the kitchen and VT editing rooms regular haunts for the presumed Napoleonic ghosts. It could be that the removal and re-burial of skeletons, when the studios were built, stirred them into action.

At the DevonAir Radio studios on St David's Hill, Exeter were strange goings on that were not scheduled. A late night presenter was totally convinced that the building was haunted. When he was working between midnight and 6 am, and he had to go upstairs to the record library, he would notice all sorts of noises and disturbances; with not a breath of moving air a door would bang shut … but they were already closed. The noises got so bad that his assistants refused to go upstairs on their own. The studios were built on or close to an old plague pit where the victims of the plague were disposed of in massed fashion, outside of the old city wall.

The cigar-smoking Mr W. Farrant Gilly was quite a showman and a much loved citizen and dignitary of Torquay. He was responsible for designing and building the former Odeon Cinema in Newton Abbot, the ABC and Burlington in Torquay and The Regent in Paignton whilst being involved with several other places of entertainment.

He had strong connections with The Torbay Cinema – beside Paignton Station – connections that seem to linger long after his death for frequently the air in the circle is impregnated by the aroma of his cigar smoke, a telltale sign of his presence. The smoke cannot be seen but its smell frequently fills the air – even in an empty cinema!

STILL ON THE JOB?

Frank of Paignton also wrote of a modern day ghost. In 1972 he was manager of a large Production Store for a very well known firm in the Midlands. The store was in a very old large building and it was July, the whole works was on holiday except for the gate keeper, himself and a man called Fred. They were stock taking some very expensive items, there were only two doors to the entrance of the store, a very large one and a smaller one. Both were always kept bolted top and bottom and locked.

Frank stood checking Fred's figures when he saw a man wearing a brown cow gown (Midlands for overall) come through the two big doors and walk up a gangway and out of sight. He knew it was impossible for anyone to open these doors from the outside. He ran down to where the man had passed and his hair stood on end, the door was bolted, but as he stood in the gangway a very cold – icy cold – started at the top of his head and slowly passed down his body. His first impression was of fear, and, as he jumped out of this thing's wake, the coldness vanished.

He called Fred and asked him to stand just where he had. Fred didn't know about the ghost but the same icy feeling crept down his body. Frank then told him of what he had seen, to be greeted by a slow smile and a knowing nod from Fred. He was due for retirement soon and had worked for this firm nigh on all his working life. He then told Frank that the very first storeman employed there had his desk at the top of the gangway and one day the manager sacked him on the spot (this was of course many years ago). The poor chap went straight home and killed himself by putting his head in the gas oven.

LOST AND FOUND

Jean from Exmouth believes herself to be exceptionally tuned in and perceptive to atmosphere. When her father died some years ago, she was obviously deeply upset as she loved him very much and knew he loved her. She will always miss him but when she has problems 'talks' to him in her mind.

A few years ago, when she was on holiday in Poole, she lost a ring of which she was particularly fond. It was unique, with a pattern of silver fern leaves joined together. She was very low in spirits at her loss but, a few nights later, she thought she heard her father calling from the sitting room. She followed the sound of his voice and found him sitting in a chair. He said, "I didn't like to see you upset about your ring, maid" (he always called her that) "So I've been to get it back for you." The next morning she thought it had been a dream but there, on her hand, was the ring. She still has it in her possession.

THE HAUNTED CITY

The ancient and historic heart of Exeter has more than its fair share of haunted happenings, possibly because people have lived and died there for more than two thousand years. It is not surprising that some of the many souls may be restless and prone to stalk their ancient stamping grounds. It could also be that the extensive urban redevelopment has disturbed their homes sparking them off into spiritual saunterings on sites where new buildings lie on old sites, some perhaps on cemeteries.

Marks and Spencer have an extremely well appointed modern store on what was formerly a Roman burial ground. There have been several strange experiences for members of staff there. A lady called Shirley, who had turned her head from her clerical work for a split second, had her pencil thrown onto her desk with great force – there was no sign of anybody around at the time.

Another worker had occasion to run up a long flight of steps in the store and reached the top somewhat breathless. Her excessive panting was matched pant for pant, by an invisible presence behind her. Whether the spirit was amicably mimicking her or simply just as out of condition as the shop assistant remains a mystery.

The most haunted part of the Exeter branch of M & S is the basement where the food hall is at present located. It transpires that quite a few ghosts are known to drift up and down the aisles.

Jackie Pullen, at one time the Manageress of the Laura Ashley shop just opposite Marks & Spencer, had an eerie experience one evening after she was called out by the police because the burglar alarm had gone off. It was early evening, between 7 and 8 pm, and when they found nothing they weren't too surprised as very often it's something as simple as a temperature change which sets the alarm off.

After the police left, Jackie had to stay behind to wait for an engineer to reset the alarm. After about forty-five minutes she realised she could hear somebody walking around upstairs. It sounded like someone pacing about both on the carpeted floor and on the wooden parts at the top of the stairs. Thinking it must be an intruder, she wisely rang her boyfriend for help, and quickly put the alarm back on. The system of light beams meant that if anything broke the circuit it would show on the system. But nothing did and when help arrived, despite a thorough search, no obvious explanation was found.

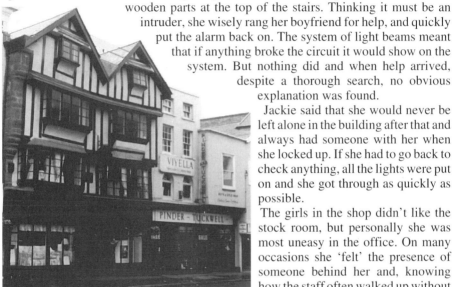

Jackie said that she would never be left alone in the building after that and always had someone with her when she locked up. If she had to go back to check anything, all the lights were put on and she got through as quickly as possible.

The girls in the shop didn't like the stock room, but personally she was most uneasy in the office. On many occasions she 'felt' the presence of someone behind her and, knowing how the staff often walked up without speaking, she said, "What can I do for you?" And on receiving no reply turned around to find she was talking to herself!

WATER, TEA AND STRONGER SPIRITS

Ghosts do some pretty crazy things. Take for instance the one which haunts Exeter's Underground Passages, a system of Medieval water conduits, which brought water into the city, under the East Gate. These former watercourses are now dry but past guides have been startled by an apparition which rode past them on a bicycle!

Judge Jeffreys was a notorious English Judge with a reputation for administering harsh sentences to those who appeared before him. His circuit brought him regularly into Devon where he was revered and feared. Although born in Kent, his ghost has elected to haunt Exeter and it is reputed that from time to time he has been seen at The White Hart Inn in South Street. Whether or not this is true you will have to judge for yourselves!

The St Olave's Court Hotel is located in Mary Arches Street, Exeter, an attractive and unobtrusive hotel sited in a former merchant's house, just a stone's throw from the busy city centre. It was built in 1827 as a private residence for Mr Golsworthy who dabbled in many activities as well as being a successful businessman. He is attributed with being the first person to use an iron piped water system in this country. His watery activities served him and the citizens of Exeter well. In 1832 the cholera epidemic claimed many victims and Golsworthy's benevolence showed in his willingness to allow the townsfolk to share his own uncontaminated water supply.

As time progressed he became sick and employed a small army of workers to service his stables and work on his behalf. It is at the converted stable block, fronting Mary Arches Street, that their mild mannered ghost appears, possibly an old stable lad. Several occupants of Room 16 have felt a presence and one guest claims that a pair of very strong arms folded around her in a gentle embrace. From time to time a male has been seen but nobody seems bothered by him as he is a friendly force.

Also very benign is the troubled soul who mooches around Tinley's Cafe in the Cathedral Close, particularly at night. He has been nicknamed 'Fred', an abbreviation of the word 'friendly' which of course he is. How could anyone who wears sandals when padding around, so as not to disturb anyone, be anything else? It is possible that this is the spirit of a former gatekeeper, at the adjacent Broad Gate, pulled down in 1823, who forgot to close the gate properly one night. An intruder got in, committed a murder of a priest and got out again. The Gatekeeper and Mayor were deemed to be responsible and were executed for their negligence.

Harry Unsworth once worked for a company called "House & Chugg" Wholesale Fruit Merchants who moved into new premises in Verney Street, the whole area having been a bomb site.

Harry recalls a story told by Mr House, and confirmed by Mr Chugg, about a haunted building at the top of Verney Street. It became a factory but had been part of a batch of private dwellings which received a direct hit during the Blitz. About ten children and thirty-four adults were killed and workmen who were clearing the site during the rebuilding, sometime about 1957, were shocked when they heard children's voices screaming and crying at 4 o'clock in the afternoon ... the same time that the place had been destroyed. The workmen downed tools and ran, and in fact did not return and a new crew had to be found. Although the sounds continued the new men were made of sterner stuff and it didn't stop them. Several people reported to the papers that they also heard children's voices when they walked passed the area during the afternoon.

In Whipton, a family who moved into a council house in Bennett Square found, to their dismay, that the house was already inhabited by an evil spirit. Although not quite so frightening as Amityville, the goings on were sufficiently scary to warrant a request from the family to be rehoused. Lights went on and off without rhyme or reason, and items, sometimes quite substantial, were moved about.

As subsequent tenants are not known to have been troubled by it, it can only be assumed that this particular poltergeist moved out as well!

THE GHOST IS COMING ...

Some ghosts like to take their time whilst out on their hauntings. One of the slowest ghosts of all time will be found at Dowrich, a large house near Sandford.

Lewes Dowrich was a gambler, a man of rude manners and one who was finally put firmly in his place by an old woman, probably the local resident witch. This old hag was upset by his antics and put a curse on him.

On 17 September 1717, in a state of blind drunkenness, his horse stumbled in a pot hole at Dowrich Bridge (that is Lewes who was drunk and not the horse). Lewes fell and died from a broken neck. The curse continued beyond the grave because it ordered him to advance towards Dowrich House at the speed of one standard cock stride (approximately six inches!) every moon (four weeks). The path was particularly tricky and, as an extra obstacle, if Lewes fell he would have to return to the starting point. As it is about 525 yards from the bridge to the House it is estimated that he should have arrived, and therefore gone to rest somewhere about the year 1973. Poor old Lewes must have surely felt quite frustrated for, after such a long journey, he was to discover that the bottom step at the gatehouse had been deliberately raised to eighteen inches in order to keep him out!

However, on a date in 1973 a hole was made in the wall before fitting a cattle grid and a new gardener saw a man seated on a horse inside the gatehouse. He was wearing a long coat and shoulder cape and bore no expression save for his eyes which were piercing. He watched him for several seconds and then horse and rider just disappeared. The gardener was completely unaware of the story and this was the first sighting in over a hundred years. As there have been no reports of sightings since, perhaps he has finally made it.

A HAYTOR HAPPENING

A foursome of friends from Bovey Tracey decided to explore some of Topsham's many attractions (many pubs) for a night of revelry and fun. However the driver remained 'dry' and the other passengers merely enjoyed a few over the odds and were still in full possession of their faculties.

On the way home they had to cross Bovey Heath and there experienced an amazing sight. High in the night sky a massive object appeared, shining brightly with a large number of lights. In sheer disbelief the people got out of their car and watched the craft, estimated to be about the same size and shape of the Eiffel Tower, move slowly across Bovey Heath towards Dartmoor. At one stage it beamed down such a bright light onto Haytor Rocks that it was lit up as brightly as daylight. The group had the presence of mind to discuss what they should do about it, knowing full well that they might be regarded as fools. However they decided to repeat the incident at the local police station.

Unfortunately the officer on duty was somewhat sceptical about the sighting, possibly bearing in mind the activities of the participants that evening. However they are all sensible people and not normally given to exaggeration or fantasy, and they maintain that what they saw was not of this world!

TUNED IN

Like me, Harry Unsworth remarks that he believes that some of us are able to receive some sort of signals from the past and one just has to be on the right wavelength at the right time. He goes on:

I must be a walking radio set tuned in at about 198 kHz. When I left the Royal Navy as a RADAR technician in 1960, TV was just getting into its stride and so I joined a company of TV and radio engineers based at Slough, but covering the South West, and one of my first jobs was to install a new set and erect an aerial at a very large Newquay hotel. Whilst tuning the set in to the only TV station available at the time, Wenvoe over in North Wales, I came across a test card that was not known to me. It was of a man's head such as the one of the ex-King Edward who abdicated, as depicted on the stamps at the time. Although I managed to get a perfect picture for some ten minutes or more, it then disappeared and no matter how I tried I just could not get it back. When I returned to our local depot at Exeter, I explained the strange picture to my boss, he listened as though with complete disbelief, and then told me that the picture I had seen had been the test card for a trial period of some twenty-four months in Ontario, Canada, but it had been abandoned about two years previously to my seeing it.

Mystery though it still is, I certainly have my own theory on the case and being trained for nearly twelve years on radio and Radar during my Naval career, I had been taught that the radio waves can be transmitted into the sky and that they can also bounce off the Heaviside Layer, which is an iron-based dust layer in the inner atmosphere, return to earth, bounce up again and so on ad infinitum until their energy is expended and they fade away. Incidentally, Oliver Heaviside, after whom the layer was named as he discovered it, was a Torquay man but he lived in Newton Abbot on the Totnes Road.

Could the signals have been bouncing for two years in space and I was the fortunate one to be at the right place at the right time to receive them? I believe so.

If that then is the case, why cannot the sounds made by man and indeed the pictures seen by his eyes also be suspended in space. Certainly we speak on certain wavelengths and each time we utter a word it travels somewhere. Those near us hear it easily but where does it go then? Spooky voices and noises could be just transmissions from the past and such things as foul deed or heroic episodes will have carried more impetus or more power. During scenes of emotion ones feelings are intense to say the least and therefore stronger signals transmitted out to the world. Are we sometimes fortunate enough to again be at the right place at the right time.

Summing up, I find that people react in one of two ways to all forms of psychic phenomena. Some listen to a 'spooky' tale with relish and believe there is a continuation of life after death, others KNOW it is a load of rubbish. To a great extent I think many events which defy logical explanation happen inside, not outside, ourselves experienced as emotion through our five senses, that the mind can travel in time – past, present and future are one and the same thing, that we already know all there is to know and our brain filters out part of the information, as much as it is good for us to know and use in every day living. With different people this varies – with some they see ghosts, some can foresee the future, all are involved in the picking up of emotions – our own or someone else's anywhere in time or space.

Strangely, since the first edition of this book, there has been some interesting feedback. Mrs Naomi Feagans from America, on holiday in Devon, was disappointed that there was no story to match the front cover illustration as she wondered if it was the same 'ghost' that appeared in the snapshot of her daughter shown here. Although clearly seen by the photographer (who was some distance away), the figure was not visible to the girl having her photo taken, alone on the clifftop. The cover illustration was actually a figment of the artist's imagination ... or was it?

Haunted Happenings in Devon